MOMNESIA

**Also by Shannon Payette Seip
and Adrienne Hedger**

If These Boobs Could Talk

MOMNESIA

a humorous guide to surviving
your post-baby brain

shannon payette seip & adrienne hedger

Andrews McMeel
Publishing, LLC
Kansas City

You're on a stroll with your one-month-old baby and you run into a neighbor. "What's her name?" she asks. Your mind fogs over. Name . . . name . . . You stare blankly at your precious child. What the heck did you name her?

"Uh . . . Winnie," you answer, eyeing the Winnie-the-Pooh blanket draped across your child. "Her name is . . . Winnie."

And for all you know, that is in fact her name.

Welcome to momnesia.

Yes, your heart is filled with the joys of being a new mom. What's running on empty is your brain. It's fuzzy, forgetful, and solely focused on the basics: food, poop, and sleep.

How can you reclaim your brain? And what can you do to survive momnesia until you're back to your old self?

You've come to the right place.

YOUR BRAIN—

Let's take a scientific look at what's happening inside your head.

This medical image shows one example of a pre-baby brain:

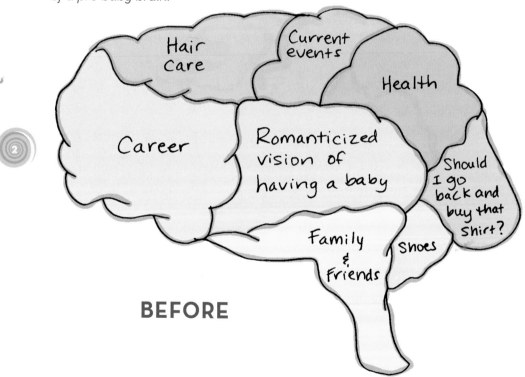

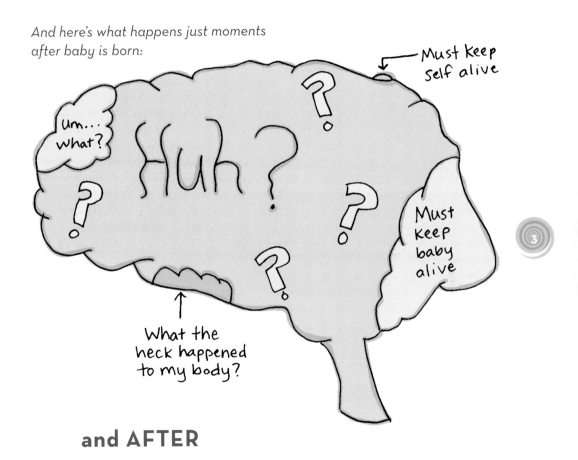

Causes of Momnesia
(That Your Doctor Won't Tell You)

1. Your brain's central processing unit froze during childbirth, and no one has pressed Ctrl+Alt+Del to reboot it.

2. Not satisfied with the big green leaf, the Very Hungry Caterpillar is now making its way through your brain.

3. Unbeknownst to you, a bunch of your brain cells are still tied up in nursery-decor issues. Was Gingerbread Bisque the right paint color? Should you have gone with Misty Shoreline instead?

4. A majority of brain cells are obsessing about the baby's name. Should you have chosen a family name? Something less new agey? A literary character?

5. Your brain is on strike, after being forced to spend too much precious time thinking about *America's Next Top Model* contestants.

6. Somehow you've landed in *The Matrix* and someone has simply shut you off.

a MOMMY with MOMNESIA ATTEMPTS to EXPLAIN MOMNESIA

Now when you have a baby, your brain begins to change in a few different ways. These changes... um... these changes...

HOW EMOTIONALLY STABLE ARE YOU?

In the last week, which of the following has made you cry? Check each box that applies.

- ☐ Baby smiles at you.

- ☐ You see a touching credit card commercial.

- ☐ You see your credit card bill.

- ☐ Hubby wants to watch the hunting channel instead of *Project Runway*.

- ☐ You realize you left wet clothes in the washing machine overnight. Again.

- ☐ You fit back into your pre-pregnancy pants.

- ☐ But wait . . . you can't zip them up.

- ☐ The dog throws up right as you get into bed.

- ☐ You see a promo for a 20/20 episode about children in danger.

- ☐ Baby outgrows 0–3 month clothes.

- ☐ A slow song with lots of guitar strumming comes on the radio.

- ☐ You discover you are out of Preparation H.

- ☐ You happen to catch a rerun of *Friends*—and it's the Ross and Rachel first kiss episode.

If you checked:

0–4 boxes
EYES of STEEL
People won't find you blubbering over an episode of *The Price Is Right* or a PB&J with not enough jam. No, you are a woman who refuses to let her tear ducts get the best of her. Except when you imagine your baby becoming a teenager. But seriously, who wouldn't cry at that?

5–8 boxes
UPS and DOWNS
Sure, you cry over the normal things, like when your husband doesn't scrape the food off the dishes properly before putting them in the dishwasher. That aside, you've got a pretty healthy emotional balance for a new mom filled with hormones.

9 or more
HELLO, TAMMY FAYE
Squirrels scurrying up a tree? An expired bag of marshmallows? You will inevitably lose it over anything that crosses your path. Might as well buy stock in Visine.

ANNOUNCEMENT!

Here's an idea: Set low expectations from the beginning by including a brief notice on your baby announcement.

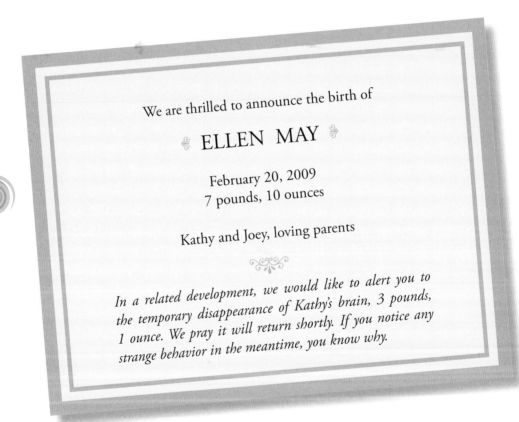

We are thrilled to announce the birth of

❧ ELLEN MAY ❧

February 20, 2009
7 pounds, 10 ounces

Kathy and Joey, loving parents

In a related development, we would like to alert you to the temporary disappearance of Kathy's brain, 3 pounds, 1 ounce. We pray it will return shortly. If you notice any strange behavior in the meantime, you know why.

GOOD GOING!

OK fine, maybe you can't quite process the front-page article in the *Wall Street Journal*. But you just gave birth! Give yourself a break and think of all the things you *can* do!

- Blink without thinking

- Distinguish between hot and cold water

- Accurately screw top on toothpaste

- Cross your arms

- Uncross your arms

- Cross your arms again

- Correctly surmise that your bra goes on top and your underwear goes on the bottom

- Toast bread and spread butter and jam on it

- Tell time on digital clock

- Snap your fingers

- Locate your baby in the crib

THERE IT IS!

Cut out this bull's-eye and stick it on your kitchen counter. Then use it as "home base" for items you're most likely to lose, such as:

- Car keys
- Baby's pacifier
- Sunglasses
- Remote control
- Your other kid

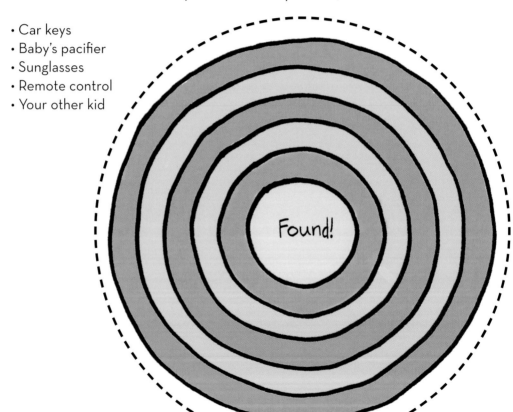

Found!

BRAIN BOOSTER

WORD SCRAMBLE

Unscramble these words:

OT _____

FO _____

NI _____

PU _____

TI _____

SU _____

MOMMY BRAIN HAIKU

Jello-like tummy

Meet barely functioning friend

Formerly named "brain"

CLASSIC MOMNESIA MOMENT

WHEW!

All right, all right. So your baby has taken your brain, your milk, and all your time. But there is a bright side. At least he didn't take your:

- TiVo remote control

- Memory of meeting Rick Springfield when you were thirteen

- Hairdresser's phone number

- Best friend's ability to listen to you vent

- Concealer

- Internet connection

- Comfy sweats that should have been thrown away years ago except they are just so comfy

- Extra-strength Tylenol

- Stack of favorite catalogs that is piling higher and higher. (You will get to them. You will!)

MOMNESIA BOOT CAMP

Get your body in shape and your brain will follow!

What the Heck Am I Doing?

Run upstairs to do something. Pause at the top of the stairs while you try to remember what you needed to do. Give up and run downstairs to check on the baby. Suddenly remember what you had to do and run upstairs again. Realize you forgot again. Repeat for an hour.

Can you make it over?

Pile Ups

Gather the bills you need to pay, papers you need to file, and magazines you need to read. Create a huge pile in a high-traffic area of your house. Jump over the pile each time you cross its path. (Note: When you can no longer clear the pile, it's time to deal with it.)

HOW SMART DO YOU FEEL TODAY?

Some days you land high on the "smarts" scale, other days . . . not so much. Where do you fall today?

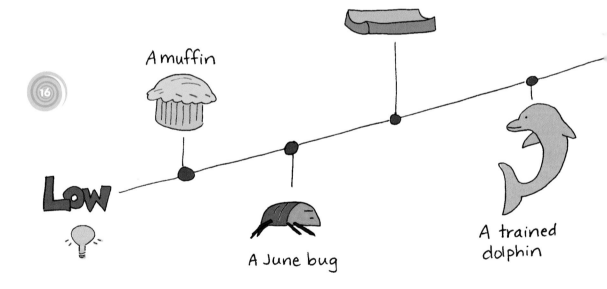

The memory foam in your baby's sleep positioner

A muffin

Low

A June bug

A trained dolphin

Assess your brain power, then plot yourself somewhere on this scale.

Good Talking to You!

Who has time or energy to talk on the phone when you have a newborn to tend to? Record this voice mail message and your friends will feel like they had a great conversation with you!

Hello? Oh hi! How are you? The baby is doing well, thank you for asking. What are you up to? Mm-hmm. Mm-hmm. Oh wow. Tell me more. Mm-hmm. I hear you. I completely hear you. Wait! Oh darn! The baby just pooped. There's poop everywhere—this is unbelievable. I have to run! I'm so glad we got a chance to catch up! Let's talk again sometime! Bye!

Note: It's a good idea to change the message slightly from time to time, lest your callers catch on to the ruse.

WHY? OH, WHY?

Instead of your brain power, why couldn't your baby have taken these things?

- Your credit card debt

- Your memory of that blind date with Teddy Finkelman

- The fifty spam e-mails that clog your in-box every day

- The strange necklace your husband bought you (which you wear out of loyalty)

- That upper-leg cellulite that, let's face it, will never entirely be gone

- That loose skin around your stomach that, let's face it, will never entirely be gone

- The expired salad dressing in the refrigerator and the expired bag of salad next to it

- Your premature gray hairs

- Your unrelenting sweet tooth

Easy Outfits

Don't waste precious brain cells deciding what to wear each morning. Instead, select one of these ready-made outfits. (Each one offers compelling benefits!)

Doctor, Doctor

Buy a pair of medical scrubs for an intriguing "on my way to operate on someone" look. Drawstring pants. Easy to wash. Completely appropriate to have strange stains all over it. And they can double as pajamas. What's not to love?

granola

No shower? No problem. Embrace the "hippie" look, complete with unkempt hair and a scarf for those didn't-get-to-shampoo days. No makeup required and sunglasses hide your weary eyes. Plus, people will admire your "Save Earth" stance.

WORKING IT

Phew! You just got back from the gym. (Yeah, right.) With this look, the more you sweat the better. Even leaking breasts will be camouflaged. You'll look like the world's most dedicated exerciser, since you'll be wearing this outfit 24/7. Even to bed.

ACCESSORY QUEEN

Huge glasses. Even bigger purse. A super-wide belt. Use a myriad of accessories to take the focus off of the fact that you are still in your pajamas.

NO SLEEP SPELLS TROUBLE

What happens when Mommy doesn't get enough sleep? Maybe once you present this chart to your baby, he'll realize the consequences of his actions.

SLEEP	CONSEQUENCES
Normal amount of sleep	Enjoy mommyhood, love your husband, exercise (or at least think about it), attempt to eat balanced meals. Feel like a normal adult.
Two hours of sleep deprivation	Become a bit grouchier. Abandon decaf coffee (even though you are still breastfeeding) and gulp down a caffeinated drink. Ahhhhh . . .
Five hours of sleep deprivation	Try to play race cars with your older child but keep falling asleep at the wheel.

SLEEP	CONSEQUENCES
Ten hours of sleep deprivation	Watch a Spanish soap opera for a half hour before you realize you don't speak Spanish. (You record it anyway to see if Luis survives the fall down the elevator shaft.)
Fourteen hours of sleep deprivation	Hold what you perceive to be a two-way conversation with your daughter's stuffed unicorn, recounting your favorite quotes from *Seinfeld*.
Twenty-four hours of sleep deprivation	Uncontrollably shout "Super Grover!" every three minutes.
Twenty-eight hours of sleep deprivation	Genuinely believe you are Laura Ingalls Wilder and hope Pa will give you a shiny penny.

WHAT YOU'D GIVE FOR MORE SLEEP

What would you give for ten hours of nighttime sleep, two months straight?

• All of your expensive hair-care products

• TiVo'd episodes of your favorite show (in fact, even your TiVo)

• All future issues of *People* magazine

• All remaining vacation days at work

• Your co-workers' vacation days

• Any forthcoming anniversary presents

• Your entire 401(k)

• Your sense of smell

• Every pair of shoes that you own

• Your appendix. After all, who needs an appendix?

CLASSIC MOMNESIA MOMENT

BRAIN VS. BREAST

In the foggy days after you give birth, a curious shift occurs. Your breasts become superior to your brain—in almost every way. See for yourself . . .

	BRAIN	**BREAST**
SIZE	Approximately three pounds on average.	Ranges from three to twenty-five pounds each, depending on time of last feeding.
ABILITY	Can retain information for, oh, about two minutes.	Can regulate prolactin, lactocytes, alveolus, and the entire milk synthesis process. In two minutes.
SPENDS ALL DAY . . .	Sending you on an emotional roller coaster.	Keeping your baby alive.
READY WHEN YOU NEED IT?	Uh . . . that's a no.	They are not only poised and ready to deliver milk when needed, they also release copious amounts of milk when it's not needed at all.

What to Do If You Start Crying in Public for No Logical Reason

Getting all choked up for no reason again? Darn those hormones! But never fear. Here are four ways you can cover for yourself:

1. Always carry a small bottle of contact solution with you. Wave it about and pretend you had to squirt some in your eyes. Exclaim: "Allergy season is here with a bang!"

2. Immediately place hands in sign language position, as if you've been signing to your baby, and your baby has been signing back to you. Dab your eyes while saying "The baby just told me in sign language that she loves me more than life itself."

3. Ask the nearest passerby, "Did you see the gas prices? They're too much to bear!"

4. Look far into the distance and simply say, "He was such a good dog."

Handy Meal-Planning Guide

Don't have time to think about food? No worries. When it's time to eat, just select one of the extra-simple recipes below. You'll be refreshed in no time.

RECIPE: *Drink with Garnish*

Fill a cup with drinking water.
Add one to two cubes of ice
(note that this is the "garnish").
Swish around a bit.
Enjoy!

RECIPE: *Crispy Delight*

Open pantry.
Locate something crispy
(cracker, cereal, expired gum).
Extract from package.
Eat with delight!

RECIPE: Peanut Shovel

Take out peanut butter.
Grab the largest spoon you can
find (serving spoon if possible).
Use spoon to shovel peanut
butter into your mouth.
Yum!

(Recommended pairing: "Drink with Garnish")

RECIPE: South of the Border

Rummage around for a can
of refried beans.
Open can. Dump beans into bowl.
Mush them up so they aren't
molded in the shape of the can.
Delicious!

(Have a few seconds to spare? Try them warm!)

RECIPE: Banana Surprise

Peel and eat a banana for breakfast.
Peel and eat a banana for lunch.
For dinner treat yourself to . . .
surprise! Another banana!

TIMES WHEN IT'S GOOD
to BE IN a FOG

There are times when momnesia gloriously works in your favor. Behold.
It's good to be in a fog...

MOMMY BRAIN HAIKU

Car keys in freezer

Next to cell phone and glasses

Breast milk thawed in purse

FANTASY VS. REALITY

Why can't mommyhood just unfold the way we fantasized? Is that too much to ask?

TIME	FANTASY	REALITY
Midnight	Sleeping.	Hear baby crying. Try to convince self it's an owl. Eventually surrender to feed baby.
3 a.m.	Reposition self in bed. Ahhh . . . so comfortable. Fall immediately back to sleep.	Hear baby crying. Stumble to crib. In sleep-deprived, hallucinogenic state, you see deceased rapper Tupac Shakur. You two converse. He's more down to earth than you thought.
9 a.m.	Open eyes and stretch. Smell coffee that husband made just for you. Mmm . . . did you sleep in again? That was so nice of your husband to get up early with the baby.	Have already been up for four hours, consumed two pots of coffee, created four piles of dirty laundry, and look like you just crawled out of a garbage bag.

TIME	FANTASY	REALITY
Noon	Lunch date with girlfriend.	Accidentally forget lunch date with girlfriend (who, by the way, doesn't have kids and has no empathy for your compromised mental state).
3 p.m.	Sleep while baby sleeps.	Feel guilty about missing lunch date, feel guilty about wanting to sleep instead of playing with baby, feel guilty about looking a wreck. Feel guilty about feeling guilty.
5 p.m.	Watch baby enjoy adorable session of tummy time.	Fall asleep face first on hardwood floor during tummy time. Drool collects in cracks of floor.
9 p.m.	Return from a romantic dinner out with husband. Perhaps some "snuggling."	Straggle to bed, unable to finish three short sentences in *US Weekly* magazine (the only "literature" your brain can possibly absorb) before falling asleep.

SIGNS YOUR MOMNESIA MAY BE CONTAGIOUS

Don't be surprised if your momnesia is rubbing off on your hubby. Signs to watch for:

• Your husband locks himself in the car in the garage and has to call you from his cell phone to ask for help.

• Your husband wears your glasses and doesn't bat an eye. (Unfortunately, the frames are magenta colored and feature small diamonds in each corner.)

- Your husband stirs up a lovely bowl of mac and cheese for your toddler, but forgets to add water to the packet of pasta and powdered cheese.

- At work, your husband ends an important sales call by saying "I love you" as if he's talking to you.

- Your husband invites the guys over for poker night, but starts shuffling the Dora the Explorer UNO cards instead.

- In total exhaustion, your husband crawls into the nearest bed and spends the night spooning your grandma.

- Your husband intends to ask his boss for a raise, but instead asks for raisins (which, oddly, he receives).

WOULD YOU RATHER . . .

Wake up to your baby crying every thirty minutes during the night or have to change a blowout diaper every thirty minutes during the day?

Cry uncontrollably throughout your entire trip to the grocery store or angrily shout your coffee order to the barista at the coffee shop?

TIMES NOT to FALL ASLEEP

When you're a new mom, it is easy to fall asleep at the drop of a hat. Just don't fall asleep . . .

BRAIN BOOSTER

WHAT'S DIFFERENT?

Can you spot the six major differences between pictures one and two?

1

2

THE MOMMY BRAIN ACHIEVEMENT TEST

SAT. GRE. ACT. Face it: You have no hope of passing these entrance exams in your current state. But there is a chance you can pass our MBAT-Mommy Brain Achievement Test. Good luck!

· ·

1. **You see a cake, candles, and balloons. What kind of event are you attending?**
   a. OK, what was the question again?
   b. Cake sounds good. When did I last eat?
   c. Is it . . . a birthday party?
   d. (Sniff.) Someday my baby will have his eighteenth birthday and move away. (Sniff sniff.)

2. **You are traveling thirty miles per hour and your destination is sixty miles away. How long will it take you to arrive?**
   a. Darn it. I forgot where I'm going.
   b. Sixty what? Who is driving?
   c. Two hours, provided I don't need to pull over and let my older child go to the bathroom six times.
   d. Why didn't I readjust that baby mirror? I can't see the baby's face! I can't hear anything! I have to pull over and make sure she's still alive.

3. **It is a beautiful day and you are pushing your baby in a stroller. What song would be appropriate to sing?**
   a. Oh my gosh, I forgot the sunscreen. And the sippy cup. And the blankie.
   b. Whoa. Why am I still wearing my pajama pants?
   c. The *Barney* theme song, since I can't get it out of my head.
   d. What was the question again?

4. **You have one hour to go to the mall and four stores you need to visit. How many minutes can you spend at each store?**
   a. I GET TO GO TO THE MALL? BY MYSELF? YIPPEE!!!!
   b. (Sniff.) I can't even look at the mall and think about what size I use to be. (Sniff.)
   c. A mere fifteen minutes at each store. But I'll take it!
   d. Why am I at the mall? Was I supposed to do something at the mall?

Answer Key:
Did you read through the entire quiz? Congratulations, smartie! You passed!

Unconventional Ways
to Relieve the Anxiety of Momnesia

La La La

Lie flat on the floor. Forget diapers . . . forget schedules . . . practice smiling at the ceiling and gesturing as you ask the *American Idol* viewers to call in and vote for you. For good measure, practice mouthing the words to the ballad you will sing as the winner. Look at that, you made Ryan Seacrest cry. You truly are the next American Idol.

Roll and Clean

Go through your cupboards and remove all canned goods that have expired. Lay the cans on their side, creating a square shape. Now lie down with your back on the cans and gently roll up and down, letting the cans massage your back.

Enjoy the knowledge that you just cleaned out your pantry. And you are getting a massage. And technically you are not wasting food. You rock.

Aaahhhh

Mix together one pound of finely chopped cucumber, one cup of lavender oil, six chilled lemon slices, and a mint sprig. Rub mixture all over head and breathe in deeply for two minutes while humming a D-sharp.

(What to expect: A glorious split second of peace while your family avoids you because you are acting crazy. You will also smell very nice.)

LOOK WHAT YOU KNOW!

Good news: It turns out your brain is retaining exactly the right information for your needs. Go, brain, go!

INFO NOT RETAINED	INFO RETAINED
What is today's date?	How old is your baby? 44 days, 10 hours!
What is the theme of "The Great Gatsby"?	What is the theme of your baby's nursery? Vintage airplanes and cars with a dark brown and light blue color scheme!
Who is the President of France?	Who is your pediatrician? Dr. Carol Turner, phone number 714-555-0101!

MOMNESIA BOOT CAMP

Physical activity can boost your brain power! Let's get moving!

Baby Carrier Butt Booster

Place baby in carrier or sling. Squat down to pick up toys, clothes, and other debris. For added resistance, wear a baby-carrier backpack and throw all the items into the backpack as you collect them.

Crib Sheet Resistance Training

Grab a clean fitted sheet (which is inexplicably a fraction smaller than the mattress itself). Ready? Now change the bedding!

Ready for a strenuous workout?

MOMNESIA MEMORY ALBUM

You religiously fill out the baby book, keeping track of all of your little one's milestones. Or at least you plan to. While you're at it, be sure to record some magic moments from your momnesia experiences. Then look back and enjoy a chuckle once your brain is back to normal.

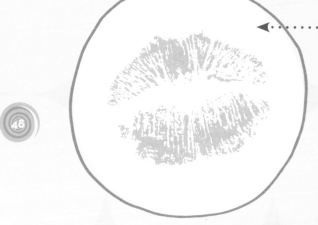

Kiss mark, displaying the lipstick you optimistically bought at the drugstore when you dashed in for diaper rash ointment. Hey, it seemed like a smart idea at the time . . . and it didn't look orange in the tube.

Picture of close friend who brought you a gift at the hospital and received no thank-you card in return.

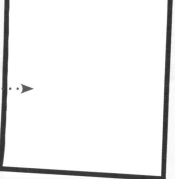

_____ Length of *your* shortest nap in baby's first month.

_____ Number of panic attacks you had during your baby's car ride home from the hospital.

_____ Number of hours you sobbed the first time you read *Love You Forever* to baby.

_____ Number of times you tried to take digital photo of baby in first month, only to realize the memory card was already maxed out.

Receipt for first item you had to purchase twice because you forgot you already purchased it.

THE GOOD OLD DAYS

Yes, you may be an emotional basket case, but a good laugh is just a memory away. Just think back on the ups and downs of your high school days, such as:

- The shirt you wore in your ninth-grade school photo.

- The time you used Sun-In to bleach your hair.

- The sheer height and width of your bangs.

- Your neon phase. Then your layering phase. Then your layering neon phase.

- Your talent for dancing the Roger Rabbit.

- Your locker display with the *Tiger Beat* cover featuring "the Two Coreys."

- Your first kiss with braces.

- Your early attempts at applying makeup.

• All the times you belted out the wrong lyrics to a Duran Duran song.

• The top-ten list you had of guys you liked.

• The mixed tape you made the summer after freshman year (which you would still listen to if only you had a tape player).

• Your acid-washed, pegged jeans with zippers down the ankles.

• "Slow dancing" by holding your partner at arm's length and swaying to and fro.

• Your involvement with the short-lived fad of licking gummy bears and sticking them to your forehead. (So rad!)

• Naming your dog Spuds McKenzie.

CLASSIC MOMNESIA MOMENT

WOULD YOU RATHER . . .

Not be allowed to sleep until you are done reading *Moby-Dick* or realize that your wedding ring is trapped somewhere in the Diaper Genie, requiring you to plow through the sausage chain of poopy diapers to find it?

Have quintuplets or spend the next ten years with no electronics (including TV, cell phone, and computer)?

53

How to Lower Your Standards

Remember: Happiness is a function of low expectations.

PRE-BABY STANDARDS	CURRENT STANDARDS
Purchase fresh produce for a fabulous dinner.	Select the "entree" in your freezer with the least amount of frost burn.
Allow yourself three hours to check out a new boutique.	Allow yourself eight minutes to shop online while breast-feeding. Never purchase anything because you plan to lose all your baby weight.
Buy a wonderfully unique wedding gift for your friend and her husband-to-be.	Show up at the wedding on the right day at the right time.
Finish your holiday shopping before Thanksgiving.	Allow your husband to do the shopping, even if it means he buys everyone a barometer.
Shower, style hair, and apply makeup before date with hubby.	Can you open at least one eye? You're good to go.

SUPERBRAIN!

Is your wimpy little brain getting you down? Focus on the brand-new powers your brain has given you!

With your post-baby brain, you can . . .

BRAIN BOOSTER

CONNECT THE DOTS

56

2
•

1 •

. 3

MOMNESIA BOOT CAMP

Come on, moms. Let's get physical!

Stroller Aerobics

Step into a deep lunge to look for the latch that collapses the stroller. Stand up. Lunge again, looking under the other side of the stroller. Stand up. Grab the stroller and shake vigorously. Fall forward as the stroller collapses mysteriously. Lift stroller into trunk. Take pulse.

Diaper Change Stretch

Jog lightly in place to warm up. Now drop to your knees and attempt to change baby's diaper when he is wiggly. Move in sync with the wild lunging and arching. Run after baby once he finally does escape.

Move in sync with the wild lunging and arching.

NIGHTS in MOMMYLAND

Why is your brain so sluggish? Because this is your typical night.

MORNINGS in MOMMYLAND

And the nights in Mommyland are followed inevitably by . . . this:

BRAIN BOOSTER

WHICH CAME FIRST?

Arrange these in chronological order, from earliest to latest.

. . . .

1. World War II   _____

    World War I   _____

2. *Sex and the City*, Season 3   _____

    Sex and the City, Season 5   _____

    Sex and the City, Season 2   _____

    Sex and the City, Season 1   _____

    Sex and the City, Season 4   _____

3. **The invention of:**

    iPod   _____

    Fire   _____

    Paper   _____

MOMMY BRAIN HAIKU

Movie date night fun

But seat more comfortable

For snoozing sans child

Double Duty

Baby stuff everywhere! Get your creative juices flowing by using some of this gear to your own advantage:

Diaper
New purpose: Cushion head when banging it against the wall in frustration.

Rattle
New purpose: Keep yourself awake in pediatrician's waiting room.

Breast pump
New purpose: Use it on your scalp to stimulate brain waves.

Pacifier
New purpose: Pop it into your family members' mouths whenever you suspect they're about to comment on your lethargic behavior.

Baby monitor
New purpose: Attach a voice-activated recorder to one end and use it to send yourself reminders.

We need more diapers. Repeat: more diapers.

Teddy bear

    New purpose: Nonthreatening item to throw at wall when you're upset that you just burned the last piece of toast.

Baby Björn

    New purpose: Transform it into a "body purse," used to carry essentials that you always seem to lose, such as keys, cell phone, sunglasses, your actual purse, etc. You may start a trend!

That annoying onesie that has, like, forty million snaps

    New purpose: Use it as a mentally stimulating game. Can you snap all the snaps in thirty seconds without missing one or falling out of sync? Bet you can't!

WATCH YOUR BACK!

Is someone trying to take advantage of you in your brain-weakened state? Be on the lookout for these ominous signs:

THE WARNING SIGN	THE DEVIOUS PLAN (BWA-HA-HA . . .)
Your husband rents football-hero-dies flick *Brian's Song*.	Hubby is exploiting your overly weepy state by introducing a sappy sports movie. Maybe if you shed tears at *Brian's Song*, you'll realize how much you love football, and you won't care if he watches *SportsCenter* all the time.
Your toddler carries empty plate everywhere.	Every hour, she tells you, "I finished my chicken" and since you fail to remember when that actually happened, you continue to give her treats.
Your sister "borrows" your expensive purse.	She conveniently "forgets" to return it, knowing that you won't remember to ask. By the time you remember (years from now), that purse will have seen better days.

Impress People at Cocktail Parties

You may only have two workable brain cells, but that doesn't mean you can't hold your own during a cocktail party. Write these sentences on slips of paper and tuck them into your purse. When the time is right, deliver your deep insight. (Then get the heck out of there before anyone responds.)

Try saying . . .

- "Well, as Gandhi once said, 'Healthy discontent is the prelude to progress.'"

- "I agree, Debi. But you know it's hard not to wonder how much of an influence spatial politics has on the geopolitical realities we're faced with today."

- "The true question is whether the laws of nature are causally deterministic."

- "As I've said before, we need to look at the effects of solar luminosity as an external effect on global warming."

- [Chuckle to yourself.] "I'm sorry, I was just thinking of line 1,322 in the poem *Beowulf*."

DISCLAIMER: Strategy not guaranteed if you compromise your two workable brain cells by imbibing alcohol.

PROOF YOU WERE ONCE SMART

One way to cheer up: Gather some items to create a small, inspiring shrine to your old brain.

Driver's license:
you passed the driving test, parallel parking and all!

Pay stub:
your brain earned money for you. And it can again.

Photo that you took:
you could operate that camera like a pro, remember?

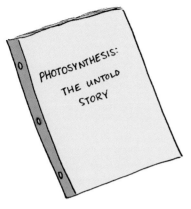

PHOTOSYNTHESIS:
THE UNTOLD
STORY

High school report:

You knew how to
spell words and
express thoughts.
(And you knew
how plants make
food.)

Wedding invitation:

You made a smart
decision selecting
your spouse.

4-ever!

Prom photo:

Wait. That is
not helpful
at all.

BRAIN BOOSTER

MATCH THE FAMOUS SAYING

Match the famous phrases or quotes to the source.

1. "Wheel . . . of . . . Fortune!"

2. "My name's Forrest, Forrest Gump."

3. "Aarf!"

4. "Chronologically you're sixteen today."

5. "Beauty awakens the soul to act."

a. *Forrest Gump*

b. *Sixteen Candles*

c. *Wheel of Fortune*

d. Italian author and poet Dante

e. Benji the dog

Answers:
1. c., 2. a., 3. e., 4. b., 5. d.
(Look at that! You knew a quote from Dante!)

CLASSIC MOMNESIA MOMENT

A BRAIN-BOOSTING SCHEDULE

It's worked quite well to have your baby on a schedule, so why not your brain? Follow this easy schedule to stimulate that sleep-deprived mind of yours:

6 a.m.   **Baby's First Feeding**
- Try to add up how many minutes you slept last night.
- Attempt to recite entire Pledge of Allegiance.
- Play games on back of cereal box.

70

9 a.m.   **Baby's First Nap**
- Name four main characters from the original *Beverly Hills, 90210.*
- Pretend to give someone directions to your house.
- Try to recall the last time you sat in peace for one hour.

7 p.m. **Baby's Bedtime**
- Recite the ABCs in reverse.
- Read *Brown Bear* with an English accent.
- While singing lullaby to baby, see if you can simultaneously remember baby's birthday, name, and gender.

3 p.m. **Baby's Second Nap**
- Remember what elective classes you took in high school.
- Name the past five U.S. presidents.
- Sharpen reading skills by reading junk mail out loud.

Noon **Baby's Lunch Feeding**
- Prepare lunch that is not frozen. Shoot for at least three different ingredients.
- Perform "Head, Shoulders, Knees, and Toes" for baby, working on accuracy.
- Decide who would be your three "friends" if you were a contestant on *Who Wants to Be a Millionaire*.

AND . . . ACTION!

Ah, momnesia. Such a wide spectrum of emotions, all hitting you at once. Wait a minute . . . you're in the perfect position to become a soap opera actress! Try this monologue on for size. Then get those auditions scheduled!

SOPHIA DELVEAUX
(your soap opera name)

(exhausted)
Oh, Rex.* I can't go on like this any longer. [Dramatic sigh.] I'm just so tired of it all.

*For added drama, refer to your husband as "Rex."

(upset)
Are those your shoes at the top of the stairs, Rex? Are you hoping I will trip, topple down, and develop amnesia, forgetting that it is your turn to change the next poopie diaper?

(suddenly break down crying)
Oh, but I will change the next poopie diaper. I will do it for you, Rex. And I will do it for [dramatic pause] the baby.

(furiously and accusingly)

But I need those good wipes! Not the cheap, horrible ones you keep bringing into this house! They smell of rubbing alcohol and despair!

(softening up)

Mmm . . . get the lavender-scented ones, Rex. The calming, calming, lavender scent . . .

(lovingly)

[Misty eyed.] Look, Rex, the baby just had a blowout, with poop splattered all the way up to his neck. Despite the stench, he is still the most beautiful baby in Bluff Valley, don't you think?

(drop to the ground; fall asleep)

BRAIN BOOSTER
CROSSWORD PUZZLE

74

CLUES

Across
1. What you just gave birth to
3. Answer to this question: Did you wear your nonmaternity skinny jeans home from the hospital after delivering your baby?

Down
1. Opposite of girl
2. Answer to this question: Would you like some time to yourself so you can sleep, shower, and/or engage in a hobby?

How to Get Organized

Some say the key to surviving momnesia is to be ultra-organized. Follow these steps to get started.

① Buy an organizer.

② Fill in your key information. (To-do lists, calendar, birthdays, etc.)

scribble scribble

③ Stuff your receipts, lists, notes, etc. into it.

④ Attempt to close it.

⑤ Fasten it with a rubber band. Admire your work.

⑥ Begin putting sticky notes all over the outside.

scribble scribble

⑦ Realize your organizer is hopelessly unorganized and, thus, useless.

⑧ Buy a new organizer!

You're Hired!

When you try to do everything yourself, you're just exacerbating your mom-nesia. Instead, try outsourcing tasks to your toddler while you tend to your newborn. For example:

. . . .

Task for Toddler: Write thank-you notes for baby gifts

Pro: Your friends will be impressed with timeliness.

Con: Notes may contain a booger.

. . . .

Task for Toddler: Schedule baby's one-month checkup

Pro: You'll actually have the one-month checkup at one month, not at two and a half months.

Con: Then again, the appointment might never get scheduled, since your toddler prefers using the Buzz Lightyear phone.

Task for Toddler: Fold laundry

Pro: At least someone is tending to the laundry.

Con: Wait, is that your maternity underwear strewn all over the front lawn?

Task for Toddler: Prepare a no-cook dinner

Pro: You may actually eat something more interesting than cereal. Yay!

Con: Does a can of pumpkin sauce, covered in salad dressing and decorated with a train track, count as dinner?

Task for Toddler: Change baby's pee-pee diaper

Pro: One less diaper you have to manage.

Con: Toddler may "change" baby's diaper into something more interesting, such as a hat.

WOULD YOU RATHER . . .

Look sharp but forget every word of a major presentation you give at work or deliver the presentation beautifully but be dressed in your old maternity sweats that have baby spit-up all over them?

Be forced to name your baby Carrie Oakey or dress your baby in a squirrel costume every day for his first year?

CLASSIC MOMNESIA MOMENT

MOMMY BRAIN HAIKU

Blueberry pancakes

My happy thought when I think

Of bill for college

PONDER THIS

Work out your brain's creative side with these thought-provoking questions!

. . . .

Ponder this: If there were a reality show based on your life, what clips from the past twenty-four hours would be used to promote the new episode?

Ponder this: If you spread all your baby gear out (clothes, furniture, toys, high chair, car seat, etc.), do you think it would it be twenty times larger than your baby? Forty times? More?

Ponder this: What was your best maternity outfit? Your worst?

Ponder this: If there were a country song written about your post-baby body, what would the title be?

Ponder this: If a crew of superheroes arrived at your door, and could accomplish anything, what five things would you ask for? (Go through your e-mail? Clean your closet? Cook your meals? Paint your toenails?)

THAT'S ENTERTAINMENT!

Good news: It takes significantly less to entertain you now.

What Used to Entertain You

- Going to a new movie on opening night

- Trying a new restaurant

- Watching favorite TV shows when they actually air

- Attending a concert

- Going out for drinks

- Hosting a party

- Escaping on a weekend getaway

What Entertains You Now

- Holding "Who's better?" competitions between breasts when pumping

- Betting on how many poops your baby will produce today

- Hearing other people's labor stories

- Dressing your infant in ridiculous hats

- Brainstorming new ways to get baby to smile

Ah la la la!

Hello! Hello! Hello!

NOW YOU KNOW

Some things just have to be learned through experience. Here's new wisdom you gained after having a baby.

HOW YOU USED TO THINK	HOW YOU THINK NOW
We won't let the baby change our lifestyle. We'll still do all the stuff we do now.	Cancel that camping trip. Cancel it now.
My friend has a baby and suddenly she can't be anywhere on time. I'm not going to let that happen to me.	Ack! OK, if we leave now we'll only be thirty minutes late. That's respectable. Oh, no— poop explosion!
We won't let our house become cluttered with baby toys.	He's done with the swing. Let's put him in the jumper. Or try the Exersaucer. Just stop the crying!
Why can't my friend ever carry on a decent phone conversation? Ever since the baby came, she can't even talk for two minutes.	What I'd give for even two minutes of adult conversation.
Why do people with kids always drag so much stuff along with them?	We're leaving for the party in four hours? I must start packing immediately.

Momnesia Music

At last! Some lullabies you can relate to.

Sing to the tune of "Twinkle, Twinkle, Little Star"

Fizzle fizzle fading brain,
How you're driving me insane.
At the store but don't know why.
What is it I need to buy?
I guess down the aisles I'll cruise.
Oh great, I'm not wearing shoes.

Sing to the tune of "The Itsy Bitsy Spider"

In the waiting room for
baby's first check up.
Oops, baby pooped.
I better clean it up.
A bag full of gear,
but nothing to wipe her.
And here is more bad news:
I forgot to pack a diaper.

The brain cells in my head go "Huh? Huh? Huh?
What is math?
What's a dog?"
The brain cells in my head are just like Dory
in *Finding Nemo*.

The tear ducts in my eyes don't care if I
cry at golf.
Or near pie.
The tear ducts in my eyes work overtime
drenching my face.

My freakin' size F boobs weigh forty pounds.
Shorter kids
can't see my face.
My freakin' size F boobs outweigh a goat.
Where is the doormat?

The hormones in my blood make me a witch.
I threw dirt
at my cat.
The hormones in my blood make me surprised
I'm still married.

LIGHT at the END of the TUNNEL

Momnesia won't last forever (at least in its current state). There is a light! Here's what lies ahead as you begin to get more sleep.

ONCE YOU START SLEEPING IN THREE-HOUR STRETCHES, YOU CAN . . .	ONCE YOU START SLEEPING IN FIVE-HOUR STRETCHES, YOU CAN . . .
• Spell the word "Mississippi." • Remember one thing you needed to do without writing it down. • Get through the day without crying out of the blue.	• Impress yourself with the patience you demonstrate. • Solve playground disputes diplomatically. • Give someone else a piece of valuable advice.

ONCE YOU START SLEEPING IN SEVEN-HOUR STRETCHES, YOU CAN...	ONCE YOU START SLEEPING IN NINE-HOUR STRETCHES...
• Complete the daily crossword, minus those few words that are so ridiculous who would ever know them. • Reclaim your witty sense of humor. • Clean the house. Somewhat.	• Ha! That's a good one.

WHAT TO EXPECT

So when does momnesia end? The short answer is: It doesn't. Sure, you will feel normal again one day. And your brain will bounce back with enhanced abilities and greater flexibility.

But your memory will probably continue to be strained. Why? Just look at all the topics, information, and obsessions your brain will be expected to retain in the coming years of mommyhood.

CERTIFICATE OF COMPLETION

To: <u>You and your brain</u>

In honor of the impressive reading and comprehension you have displayed throughout the course of this book.

(If you happened to just turn to this page randon well . . . we are in a generous mood, therefore y are also honored. We are not sure for what, b we hope you enjoy your honor nonetheless.

Congratulations to you and your brain. You h conquered the mighty mountain of momne and are on your way to wonderful things.

Do you have a momnesia moment to share?

Tell us at:

www.momnesiathebook.com

(Don't worry . . . we all forget to wear our shoes to work
from time to time. We won't make fun of you.)